for Quinton

THE HOUSE OF NOBODY HOME

Nancy Carol Moody

FUTURECYCLE PRESS

www.futurecycle.org

Library of Congress Control Number: 2016939540

Published by FutureCycle Press
Lexington, Kentucky, USA

ISBN 978-1-942371-00-7

CONTENTS

I. THE SWALLOWED HOUR

II. STRADDLING A FAULT LINE

III. Wheel Marks in Stone

Acknowledgments

I. THE SWALLOWED HOUR

In the Beginning

Apple, tell me
your name.

Spell it with alphabets
I can imagine.

Hand signs will do,
those flapping wings,

bluster a verb
I long to bite into.

Oxidation burns
only part of the story.

Allow me a slice
beyond your skin,

bitter, bursting
with flesh.

SUITE: HOUSE, STORM

Night into night, the house flinches
beneath wind- and rainfall. Blister
cresting the slurried soil, it is
its own umbrella, overturned tuna can
straining against a gutter eddy,
the last pliosaur's unproven shell.

*

The atticless house shudders
under hoof-fall. That dogged ark,
its sodden inhabitants—all upended
without ceremony, the roof-skin
a membrane a dispassionate god
would puncture freely with his staff.

*

Fascia, sill, doorframe: the watered
colors flee, bleeding into tooth
and ground, penciled guy-lines
a vanishing tether. The house exists
where the rain does not, a frisket
mere fingertip could rub to crumble.

AFTER THE CHURN

after Basin 4, *a work on paper by Robert Tomlinson*

this watery whirl, wrung into particulate.

Flesh heap, bone-dump, spawn of wreck and batter—
what is no longer
amasses in the shallows

the breach unseen for all that fills it.

Red notes singsong just beyond reach, hover,
diminish,
fall to fleck.

Floaters on the brink nudge and moan
unblinking, translucent.

All is tulle.

The seafloor swirls
with indecipherable tracery, messages scrawled
on fogged glass.

Gray eddies into gray, and then
a calm.

How swiftly they row in, the boats of sadness.

AND NOW MY MOTHER AGAIN

the back of her, boarding a bus.

A snag in her blouse, no,
a tear in the seam where petals of flowers
pinch into themselves.

She hasn't set foot in my dreams
for more than twenty years;

then, that wall she stepped so easily over

as if it were a simple pasture fence.
And when I ran to look
nothing but wind-carved dunes I plunged

headlong into, my mouth
filling with sand.

O Mother, how is it that what remains
is the grit of you
sifting through my fingers?

Once there was a beach, waves and salt spray.
Tar balls gummed to the soles of my feet,

flat and black as Sunday pancakes.

The sand crabs I brought home
in the yellow bucket
stunk up my room with their death.

How you cleared out the smell
with rags you shredded with your teeth,
then promised me

one lily to lay across the troweled grave.

Scentless flower whorled like a seashell, no sound
of the ocean in its ear.

What was it you longed for those arid years,
when my mere reach could pull you inside out?

And still I cannot stare

into a tide's carnival pool
without seeing that starfish blessed with six arms;
beside it, another, left with only four.

Even then, a lesson in the averaging-out, a limb
the price of a limb.

And now the back of you, boarding a bus,

a woman of apparent substance
inhabiting this city I do not recognize.

How your hand reaches out
to grasp the rail, letting it support
the whole weight of you,

that hole in your blouse, the one small gasp
of flesh I'm allowed.

QUENCH

What flares us to couple,
burns us there?

One, raw meat, hissing on the spit;
the other, aspic
slipped too soon from its mold.

Despite walnut shells, blur of hands,
passion's sleight of smoke
and mirrors,

we know how this will all turn out:

a blear of slickness no one wants
to swab, mophead stained red
for years to come.

*

Bayou nights.

It was you I had, specter
rising from breathless heat,

my swampland.

Such inconsequential shine,
petty tendernesses,

these bits of scar
persisting beyond mosquito bites.

Big as thumbnails, they lit
our backs like rows of tacks,
left flaming hillocks

we scratched around.

Our fingers wrote erasures, tracings
white hot against raging flesh,

bright tracks through fire
which embered our spines, fused us.

This was before the melt.

Aubade at Seaside, Rent into Fourteen Lines

Cloudlift   then
          an exhalation of sky.
On the froth-lipped hardpack—
      one dominion fluxing into another.
Crustaceans scribbling devotions,
     splayed shell of mollusk
         an unbidden valentine.

Just yesterday   vespers,
        the plates cleaved in stalemate.
Pulver of sand   scale   salt
     the burn fervid beneath our feet.
Foam etching an unbroken scrawl,
     foreshadow of itself, itself
        sidewinding into the gloam.

Yellow

Morning spreads like an omelet
across the eastward sky.
Blades of green hiccup from the dirt,
blister into narcissus.
The caterpillar escapes
the chrysalis, emerges a monarch.

Nyjer in the feeder, house-
finches flit aside for gold-.
Leaves of a dry late summer
fade toward fawn and swirl.

Beneath their roof of dermis
the macrophages carry on
their quiet occupation,
ambering down from purple
my bruised and onioned flesh.

What isn't tipping toward yellow?

I see myself in the mirror
and want to run like hell.

Missive

There's a letter in the mail that didn't mean
what it said
when it left the house.

Carrier pigeon tangled
in the ribbon of no-turning-back.

Snapping turtle in the postman's tray

riding in on a stamp
with a flag named *Forever.*

The little toy truck toddles down the lane
on the right side
of the cinematographer's split screen

carrying its happy load
of wishbooks and baked cookies.

Musical notes twirl in the trees.

And now from the left
the camera zooms in on that single envelope,

black script darkening
as it edges
near delivery.

Too late, screech the wheels.
Too late, slams the mailbox lid.

Is it any wonder
I keep looping

through this video of the sinkhole,

the acres of cypress towering one instant
on the brink
and then in the next

vanished into the abyss.

Item Found in a Dresser Drawer

A watch,
left by my mother and broken—
as were her all.

(She kept the jeweler in business for years.)

She would do the same
with mine—break them, that is—

wrapping my newest timepiece
on her wrist on Christmas
or birthday mornings, the bright

hands stalling, fixing the instant.

Halted time tucked gleaming
back into the velvet-

lidded box until the repair
shop opened
for business the next day.

I thought

that was the only death in her,
my soft mother, killer

of watches. Pocket, wrist, locket—
she could stop them all.
But beneath,

neither in ticker nor muscle,
rocked in the sling of breast-flesh,

another sort of chronometer loomed.

How slight a movement
of one hand
would it have taken to admit

the lump when it was new
as a stopwatch, pristine

in its pouch and still under warranty.
But no—

by then she had grown
accustomed to it, you see.
The box.

Its snapped-closed lid.

ARCS OF DETACHMENT

The father wanders off in the night.

There are theories,

just as cows ease their heaviness through pastures,
invisible only to stars.

Downwind of the gate: handprints in quicksand,
a slide rule missing its case.

Boomerangs shear the color from clouds.

Carnival sweets turn the children's mouths blue.

Deterrence would have been good advice,
elasticity a potion to come back home to.

An effigy clings to the flagpole.

The square root of *if only* is not factored for shame.

The constellations realign by increment,
December no more than a matchstrike away.

Snow Is Accumulating Rapidly

The Weather Channel—Denver, Colorado
for Colette

Sky pink.

Dander
on the soft shoulder, I-70
kinking

through the passes
like a ribbon
pulled

through a girl's hair.

White into
white, a bread truck barrels down
the slow lane,
icy loaves sliding
off the roof of the cab.

You've chosen this existence on the high plain,
though questions
pile up as

overhead
the onion sacks
blacken—

> *When will the grasses howl for placation?*
> *Will the morning, too, be construed from etched glass?*

Drift against the basement windows.

Shadows notching

up the playroom
walls.

And you,
with your dream of warm feet, pushing
against

the dog's frost-spangled belly.

You think of your father, cracking
bones to make his living—

no such relief now
as you sit fixed in lotus, positioned

for the long haul.
Waiting

has never been your long suit,
but now you're dressed
to the nines in it, whether

the fit is ill
or not.

Once upon a time
there was a girl

who would ride her dapple mare
up to the high crest

and sit
looking over the ridge
to the valley below,

flurries swirling
the leather of her boots.

She didn't notice the ice-scaped pinnacles.
She never saw

the coppered hills,
how they
greened

in their waning.

Another Poem about Winter (1)

Winter squeezes so hard
in these mountains

that even the ice cream
won't stay in its carton.

Sky a Spirograph of cirrus and switchbacks
mean tire chains

clattering in the wheel wells.
Pine pitch flash-frozen to soles of boots.

Lid held firm, and still
it takes forever for anything to boil.

At peak of season, there comes
the luxury of heated conversation,

nothing being argued into thin air.
How it aches to breathe—

lungs so emptied
the brain gets pulled down into them.

ANOTHER POEM ABOUT WINTER (2)

The snow's a broken record
on these hairpins at 28 below.

Arrowed yellow signs hieroglyph cautions
the nerve-wracked can't glimpse.

Wiper blades swish-swish
over false promises of easy sleet.

Recall the salesman, waving
his wand over the car's black hood.

Beneath, hose like a missing guardrail.
Fan belt crumbling like mountainside.

If a key turns in the ignition
and no one's there to rev the engine,

can horsepower still drive you
over the cliff?

The clutch is holding,
but what?

O to ride a magic carpet
spun from Zero-G.

And this prayer: May there be icing
on nothing but cake.

Patsy on the radio singing
"I Fall to Pieces,"

and she did.

Motel

Edward Hopper, Western Motel

The room is too warm.
They always are.

Chalk begins here.

As does the deep of scarlet.

Nothing is left
unmade.

Let's say the Buick is not hers

but that it has come for her.

You could at least
help her

with her coat.

Anywhere, DST

Month of springing forward, yet
that hour—

where does it fall?

Beautiful woman of March
with a gap in her teeth.

The moon, unfazed,

retreating into its phases,
and all my disappearances

so easily explained away—

except for those times
when I was there, but not really there.

If we could choose one god, which would it be—

a sunset, with its pulled-taffy, citrusy obviousness?
the lit cigarette at the end of desire's alley?

that swallowed hour?

By daylight
no one will be left to remember

you had ever been here.

II. STRADDLING A FAULT LINE

ADAM: THE SEQUEL

This mount of apples,

and when I provoke it—
an entire garden balmy with cider.

Also, that otherworld smell—
the early sweetness of decomposition.

O to have been known by so many names:

Cameo, Delicious, Candy Crisp.
Pippin, Greensleeves. Topaz, Gala, Beauty of Bath.

Bruises to be cut or eaten around.
And its seeds

the sort of bitterness that can be swallowed whole.

Knife to taut skin and the voluptuous split.
The throaty namesake, its rise and fall.

A worm once made a carnivore of me.

And then that old woman in each one's dried self—
so many faces of Eve.

The heft of Rome apples,
one in each palm,

weighs like imagination.

CONTROLLED FLIGHT INTO TERRAIN

This mountain, obscured by cloud.

It stood here all this time,
waiting, as it was bound to wait.

We were intractable, too:
to believe in a cloud's other side
was to believe in more cloud.

How easy it seemed, the reaching up,
altering the flow of chilling air.

A fingertip could snuff the light's tight beam.

Instrumentation, we thought, was overrated;
pressurization, a roar we willingly slipped into.

Cloud eases up and over and around,
the thinnest scrim covering its tracks:

there are some who would call this faith.

When we hit, we still could not see through it.

ECHOLOCATION

Threw out a click, an aimless
tongue-snap, and it came back
as tree: lean and feathery
on the high note, wall-solid
and thick on the low. Not
kickback exactly—more like
soft bounce off straw pile
suggesting the form that lies
beneath. Rods and cones
make a hideous noise,
20/20 a false positive
to measure oneself against.
Click click click. Click click.
The metronome's tick
twins itself. The singular bark
of the night dog keeps its own
company on the long circuit home.
Where you stand is entirely
dependent on what might make
its way back to you. So little
has been said about the whisper
returning to the ear as song.

THE HUMAN DOUBLE HELIX DOES NOT SPIRAL INFINITELY

Again, a tuft
of yesterday freewheels past and my fingers
grasping

apprehend *elusive.*

Once, confusing martingale with nightingale,
I made nonsense of a sentence.

Memory can be that, too: a sentence.
As in: subject, verb, object (direct or indirect).
As in: without parole.

The 5 a.m. jogger reflecting head lamps
believes it's her own sum she's saving

but has no means of calculating mine
(thud of figment eternally glancing off my hood).

I have snapped

the bones of Leghorns with my hands.
Watched a body tossed across fire.

For a time I had a man who painted
one side of his house every year,
the work forever current.

I cipher such a project of myself: never done.

To the invisible squirrel
auguring through the soffit:

I understand now you're not trapped
inside the attic.

No. You're scheming ahead a second way out.

Ajar

for Lynn

A door open slightly
inside a house where nobody's home.

No malevolence
intended: this is not about ghosts
or screaming

birds of prey or everything I ever regretted

returning to skim the skate pond
with glissandos of ice.

It's just that there's an order to things—

who fills the feeder
by spilling seed on the ground?
poisons the fish then drags out the seine?

One can argue the logic
of growing melons in the shape of cubes

so no space is wasted in the shipping.

But consider the cost.
Not to mention the rot when the flatbed collapses
under the weight

of all that conformity.

A vacuum leaves tracks in the carpet
saying *I was here and this is what I needed to do.*

Like this door, ajar. Yet another closed behind it.

What we keep hidden.
The gape we leave for it to slip through.

Name Change

for M.C.C.

For a time I was called something
and then no longer.

Echo absent its own ears to return to.

Once I dropped
a pebble down a canyon, stood
at the brink

waiting for the splash.

It came, though
not in the way I'd expected, which is

what we might say about most
stories

we take on

just for the chance
to brag to our friends that we'd

known the ending all along.

If you
stand in a stand of trees, there's

a shushing sound

like a whisper
whispering back to itself.

A plink lands in the creek,
which is just the place a plink belongs.

You gave me a name

and then you left me
on my own.

I, the daughter you can't own.

SPARROW

The sparrow
that just slammed into the window
was aiming straight for herself.

Torpedo crumpled in its cardboard tube.
Mirror at the end of an endless hallway.

Wall of glass.
House of cards.

Ricochet and stun.

How many times
did I dive
right into a pool emptied of water?

The fact of no blue
should have given something away,

but O how I wanted it
and believed

that was enough.

Desire is a grenade
planted beneath the carousel.

The horses. The lions. The pink pigs
on their twisty gold stems
frozen in monotonous flight.

The ticket-taker shushing everyone off the ride.

But then, that one boy
left clinging to a pole,

and his father—half comfort,
half shame—
trying to pry him off.

The end of the world in a pin
that may
or may not have been pulled.

The end of the world in the boy's screaming.

I tell you now, *I lied.*
I lied about everything.

There were always two sparrows.

One finding the glass and glancing off.
The other wanting what it saw there,
shattering through.

A Forest Argument Leads to Sea

Boots seeking traction on moss-slicked stones
don't heave themselves one in front of the other
because they're looking forward
to the going-back—

such meticulous muscling up the forest path
presupposes a terminus. No, that's not right—
a fulcrum's more like it, a place to balance
before deciding where next to head.

Eventually the firs in their scraggy coats
start looking like surrender. A significant portion
of ambient roar is no longer attributable
to held breath letting loose through treetops.

Whisked-aside ferns grow crisp around the edges;
thermals crisscrossing dank humidity
give way to sting and face-slap—
that's salt air scouring the headlands!

And then this—blue running headlong into more blue.
A wild strawberry surprises
with its almost-painful pucker of red;
green flat fans of leaves runnel down basalt castoffs

flanking the dry crumble underfoot.
What leads to the brink has been ground down.
Here, at the limit, when boot-toe strikes surface
there remain just two possible outcomes: kick of sand

spuming a parody of sea spray or hard slam
into cliff wall, geologic equivalent of the glottal stop.
But isn't this what we've wanted all along—to have it
one way or the other, nothing in between?

I'm Not Like You Think I Am

This late November light—
liquid minerals sluicing through panes,
puddles gridded impossibly to walls.

This close to evening,
angles and physics preventing
the presumptive pools on floor.

Even the cat understands
the need to move on—
he soaked up his piece earlier in the day
when it still contained
a useful warmth.

Out in the field
beyond the window—
a woman, wandering the weeds
in her dark long coat.

The dog she keeps for company
leaps in arcs above tops of fading grass.
The woman looks to her feet,
walks her tighter
and tighter circles.

—If you believe the passing light
says something about the way
a day can turn itself inside out

—if you think a woman walking
by herself in a field
is loneliness

you are wrong.

AND THE WREN BEARS TO HER NEST ANOTHER TWIG

i

Furthering, furthering—
feet by habit
by memory
stepping one in front
of the other
perforating
bisque
once glossed
so easily over.

ii

Wax has a way
of melting
around the heat
of a thing
figuring its own shape
onto a shape
wicking
a glowing distortion.

iii

This ticking could be
clock, metronome, rice
hitting sidewalk, patch
of stickiness on a shoe or
    drip
          drip
      drip

iv

Pullover slipped
its hanger, not
seen, not missed, then
resurrected
from among the coats and
day arcing all over again.

CALIFORNIA

Biology delivered me into you—
tidal surge
and those desert hills that bucked

against the bald sun beckoning *ride me ride me.*

Desert—both sand
and the line drawn in it.

Landscape so dry my mouth couldn't spit it out.

Lakes shivering in the wells of mountains
like women readied
for something

to dive their blue chill depths.

There were rumors of gold to the north.
I followed them

beyond a valley falsely green and the stink

of rice flats and a sulfurous spew that no one
bothered to listen to.

The earth with a story it was hell-bent
to tell
rocked so hard that

a lightning bolt lay flat down against it,
splitting

so wide and deep the floor

that forever became a fall
there wasn't rope enough for.

In all my life
I'd never loved anything that wouldn't
hit bottom.

Once, I flung my arms
around a redwood's flaming girth.

That was a moment,

and then the thing
burst out of me like prayer—
bark-scrape and bedraggle and

it never entered me
that there could be such a dream
as the letting go.

Map seared by salt,
I conjured promise

in a place etched *Eureka*.
Tasting the distance, I traversed the bitter
frail edge.

Whatever tide
meant deliverance from there,

it couldn't unearth me.

NAMING

The pond that formed in the meadow after the rain—
we gave it a name.

A name is not an easy labor. It is as difficult as white.

Indigo ink, alphabets on skin spelling old loves.
Erasure, too, a thing to regret.

Everywhere, fingerprints. No powder to reveal.

In the lining of your pocket, initials embroidered,
needlework insisting on its own complications.

In this shy room, a flush of neon pinking the margins.
A trickery of black paint, gas, bent glass.

Smoke slips from your mouth, the story's last draft.

I hold a shell against my ear.
All names, yet only the one, murmur in the swirl.

A match blazes the book of where we have been.

Your finger, drawing a line down my back. A dot.
Exclamation mark on what we name our final naught.

SPRING BOULEVARD

The doe, dead by the side of the road,
causes the snag of me to tighten,

all my griefs yet to come
foreshadowed by this carcass caught in the act
of minding its own business.

Did the doe see the car before the car became the wall
that slammed smack into her?

Sometimes all you do is stand in one place

and bricks come crashing down
from a fourth-floor window.

Right now your feet could be straddling a fault line.

There's a crazy rope of wind
whistling through the mountain pass, and
it's yanking me

in a direction I hadn't planned to head.

I tighten my grip on the wheel.

And the doe—
the doe's already fading into the distance behind me,

her astonished belly
exposed, blazing like a white light.

In Which I Explain to You About the Tongue

The tongue is the only muscle in the body connected at just one end.

I've seen dogs like that, tethered
to a clothesline in a yard, their days strung to thirst and yelp.

The case can be made for other creatures: the cobra, for instance.

Tongue—slick
little engine of meat and slaver,

just the sort of trick a pissed-off god would play,

his patsy doomed to an eternity of *not-quite:* always
reaching, always

pulling back. Desire
never quenched by one thing or the other.

And then you grab it with your teeth.

Hang on like that lamb
refusing to be dragged to the holy table.

When at last you let it go, I recoil. Then snake it out again.

ABLUTION

A stone in my pocket, rough-edged—
I haven't been worrying enough.

More evidence—someone's scrawled *WASH ME*
on the rear window of the car.

Small vandal—his finger accomplishing
what the idols of guilt and virtue could not.

Here I am at Jiffy Wash—
the car's being dragged by a chain through the cloths.

I'm in it to the sopping end—
this drain too narrow for gods, for rocks.

SCAR

At age 5, I put my hand
to a wall

(I was only trying to
steady myself)

and crushed good-bye
the bee thereon.

My first remembered kill.

The stinger
pulled so swiftly out.

Such
a small thorn I

carry on my palm
this life.

EIGHT

Before infinity
before the tipping

there posed the eight.

Eight pinches a teaspoon.
Pounds of cheese a clove.
Place settings to a box.

Sleipnir of Odin.
Arms of the squid.

Eight queens puzzle.
One fat lady.

Skate a figure.
Pieces of.
Section.
Crazy.

Zero kiltered off
with a midriff twist.

Equilibrium holding
upright or prone.

O hourglass—

O lorgnette—

Look what you've done.

III. WHEEL MARKS IN STONE

REINCARNATION

To come back
(to have come back)

as something kinder

would be
(would have been)

a kindness.

Blue glass dish for the finches
to splash in.

Middle C ribboning through a din.

And still I cannot cross the plains
without seeing on every barbed fence

a boy tied there.

Headlamp newly on or soon to be
flicked off.

Next time will be moths.

A mausoleum untended
is seepage.

Sometimes to melt is the only way out.

Let there be one tool precisely milled
for the doing. Or undoing.

To return as apple.
To bleed nothing but clear juice.

CANDY DISH

Temptation laid out on a divan of glass.

Such color. Such abundance. Such
shameless sweetness.

We could be talking about love.
Or possibility.

Danger, even—

the flaming cars, slapped faces, the bright-banded
muscle coiled in the corner.

A helicopter
shot to fireworks in the sky

and children unfurling
to catch the sparks, so exquisite

in their extinguishment.

Just try. Try
to take only one.

So recent in the setting-out
and already

how they cannot help but cling to one another.

CREAMER

Knocked over

and from a distant room a mother calls, *Don't cry
over what's spilled.*

There are mops. Rags. Machines
for laundering table linens.

Boulders downstream for battering
our dirty wash against.

What's done is gone, the consonant shifted.

And the mother doesn't understand.
It had been cream held there.

Here now she comes, bearing her cloth.

Box of Rocks

Halfway beneath a table,
lid torn back,
$2 scrawled in black marker on the side,

these yard-sale rocks, heavy
as regret.

Two dollars, the price of an accumulation.

Scumbled with mud, collaged
in dry leaf, bits
of cobweb, the lost wings of insects,

they glint
like old loves, rugged stars.

They too had lives once,

arrived in this unlikely place
because someone spotted a moon in them,

because a hand reached out and said, *You.*

O to have been the one chosen,
the hurried heartbeat of that.

Dimple, curvature, an angle
of polish. A palm that curled itself
around our shape,

and in its closing became our shape.

To have come through the tumbling.
And then, this hardness

we were shouldered into, the dismal
weight of us.

Lid folded down,
the cardboard darkness,

our hearts ticking, one against another.

When They Ask About My Face

I will say something
about snow, the skittered tracks
of a hare just prior to the hush.

I will say wind bores
salt into sea-boards,
taut rope burns a furrow,
leaf rust in spring autumns elms.

Hoarfrost bit by hobnail.
Meadow after the scythe.
The dory's barnacled hull.

A peppermint held
too long against the palate.

When they ask about my face,
I will say that even a trodden carriage
leaves wheel marks in the stone,
that shrapnel can flare
a staggering tattoo,

that left to their own devices,
sparks of midnight fireworks
will carve ferocious trails
into the black wax of the sky.

BUTTER KNIFE

You've tried, but this knife
doesn't cut it—

the mustard. To the chase. To the quick.
And dried. And run. And

hasn't this been the story of your life—
fragment and disconnect, lever and blunt blade?

At last—at least—you've managed
to wrap your hand around it.

Though you should have known by now
not to expect otherwise—

the iced resistance,
bits and pieces congealing in a pile.

Always this dull thing
you spread yourself thin with.

REGENERATION THEOREM

for Q.H.

You fashioned shoes of clay
   for the downside-up and two-
      pronged stick, set him headless

     on your porch to make
   his morning's stillborn stroll.
It's not new news that a chicken

will syncopate even after
   his brain's been lopped, but
      do you know about a lizard

     at large in, say, the entry hall,
   how if you snatch him by the tail
his body will unfasten

to make its intrepid getaway?
   The stump will regenerate
     to an approximation

     of its bygone measure,
   but what about that
wayward tail, unexpectedly

absent its choreographer and
   twirling disconcerted figure
      eights across the parlor floor?

     Both sides of the lizard's
   mortal equation total
to the same earthly sum—

what's lost or left behind
    will calculate some means
        to reinvent itself.

        That inverted biped, dead
    wood propped on the bench
near your door—one day

you spied a grounded bird
    who'd found on it a shoulder
        to talon to as makeshift perch.

    The next time you glanced,
    they both had flown.

MILL CREEK AT PLAINVILLE

The water in its ancient turning
churns its foam over jut and boulder,

augurs new and infinite departures.

This, a story that's been told before—
upstream not a place

but a way of pushing against yourself.

A rock does not bear a name,
but knows enough to say, *Make something*

of yourself by resisting me.

Water like an eel, sidewinding the current.
Water like cling wrap's crinkled obfuscation.

Water like a whistle, boring through.

Eventually something has to give.
The unimpeachable leaf will tell you how

the water only takes.

SCRIPTURE

River bridge at night lit red,

the spans
striking a callous alphabet.

Your name—

I wrote it first in blue
when we were
otherwise, when we

were letterpress,
our best lines inked

in meticulous relief.

And then I penned you
in the margins

again and again
until you became just one more
meaningless scrawl.

Handwriting on the wall,
the ages dutifully note.

Asterisk and swirl—

our whitecaps
inscribe the current.

Permanence Being Art Not Science

Five parallel contrails,

birdless wires
tensioned across the morning sky.

Musical staff and orange-blue notes.

A wintered storm hauls itself over the horizon;

you, the silhouette
I barely recognize, kick and dangle

from that everlasting cliff, knuckles
slip-knotting

the loosing ground above.

Icicles form like salvation, damp
slickness to muscle and good-luck against.

Prepare for frostbite. For burn.

Did no one ever tell you the ice might be dry,

evaporating into air
even as you wrap your cold torsion around it?

Cinquain of life ropes
dissolving into the rippled wake.

Prepare for gravitational pull.

If you listen to the blue
for a streak of birds, you can

know it's possible to be saved.

CODA

after a photograph by Chema Madoz

Rain as bobby pins slanting into a surf-storm of hair.

Such whimsy. Such spectacle.
Cinematography viewed through a porthole mat.

But before this—that film I watched.

A calamity at sea.
The ship's terrible crack and list.
(Of course it was a storm. It always is—the electricity,

the flailing rage.)

And the inevitability beyond—no *dénouement*
of an orderly sinking.

Instead,
whole bodies wracked
to rafts of wreckage the size of arms.

No need here to belabor the details—

we've all been
a version of the havoc celluloid has to offer.

Yet there it was.

Predictable on the screen in the rumbling dark and
it caught

me anyway—
the girl's fingers rent like splinters from the board, her curls

tangling with the wild and stylized sea.

BOATS IN STASIS

after E #12, *a work on paper by Robert Tomlinson*

the sea a travesty of ink.

White whale held in permanent dive, chunks
bitten out of its hull.
Swimmer locked in Australian crawl.

A woman blows a trumpet, the instrument obscured.
No, she's screaming into her hands.

I was a girl like that, suspended
in a pooling thickness I wanted

to believe was grace.

But just below the watermark, my every skiff
upended, black half-moons

of eyelids, forever closing.

Hopeless in the murk—
life ropes thin and fanciful as string.
Postage stamps for letters never to be written.

Ghost reflections rise like bubbles,
inverted boats I scratch out with my battered nib.

THREE VIEWS FROM THE HARBOR

The indifference of gulls says something about flight.

What's not said about air is that it lifts as surely
as it can slam.

O pickpocket wind.
How you plundered us for wings

we never knew were there.

*

Different, this lighthouse
from its rivershore kin.

River says it's safe, maneuvering here.
Ocean warns, *Steer clear.*

Still the gulls circle. Barnacles encroach.

Wind ropes a nest composed atop a buoy.

*

Vessel strung with nets and buoys and

the sea like forgiveness
calm-surfaced beneath it.

Hull fraught with barnacles below the waterline.

So much entanglement.
So much hope.

STILL LIFE WITH IMMACULATA

A version of myself
is lying
in a tub of bath water,
circa
sometime long before
now.
The water, when I enter it,
is hot,
but soon becomes
precisely
the tepidness that is me.
Eyes closed,
I can only be certain
the water
is still there by shifting
my body
slightly, a telling ripple
rising
to the harrowed vee between
my legs.
The wake in its temperance,
anointing me
so instinctively, delivers
a touch
I should have always known.
You can
guess at what comes
next—
the inevitability of the cooling-
down.
The water's icy ardor.

What if
I were to tell you
that this
is the reason I invented
fire?

SANTA MONICA FREEWAY, 1970-SOMETHING

Such a thing was possible then—

a car broken down
on the inside lane and someone in the right
place, right time,

pulling up behind, hitting
the flashers,

and climbing out to help
push it toward the shoulder.

Call Box never far, eastbound or west.

I know,
because we did just that—

the sun hazed
and low to water, headed
for its usual bar,

pavement so young
it still grooved white.

These days the freeway's an Etch A Sketch
of tar patch—horizontals, verticals, shaky
diagonals. You could

zigzag on them for miles and never
even cover one.

Small is four lanes stopped and waiting.
Recollection, too (both the small and the waiting).

The cars huddled behind their headlamps as we shoved.

You'll remember we were headed east.

I'll say west.

GRIEF

for J.R.

Someone took a straw, blew holes in all the clouds.

Now this strew of cotton, a thing for birds to gather,
take with them to the nest.

Upside-down thimbles puff across the sky. Overhead a pig, floating
on a skateboard. In the distance a mouth, tongue of vapor sticking out.

A plane flies left to right. Disappears. Emerges.

The blue sky yawns, dispatching its flock to the margins,
a hole dead center, like an ocean. Sooner

or later, something comes to fill it:
fill it   fill it   fill it

TABLECLOTH

You know that old trick—
grasping one edge

and jerking it so fast and clean

that the plates
and glasses remain in place,

just an afterthought

of shimmer
left to record the stun.

We think of it as magic,

but what hasn't been yanked
from beneath us—

and still we're left standing.

OF A THOUSAND OTHER THINGS THAT TURN UP

a cento, from Quinton Hallett

If there is a fresh pear on the counter

if spring blares magnolia and forsythia
along the verges of night

there is no possibility of betrayal.

Walk into the woods.
If volume is ever to be increased or diminished

stealth is your best suit

refracting too much noise and light
invisible to everyone but you.

Listen to me tap the old tunes sotto voce.

To measure or contain is an insult
where metal corrodes just short of bursting.

It might be a bullet in the chamber or a blank

or sometimes, pendulous clouds.
Yet every condolence left beside the bridge.

At first, one of anything marries the void.

If there is a feral woman
forget that old myth, tough as dried fruit.

You won't last an hour in open air.

To name the body of water.
To cover innocent shrubs before they clench.

To wrap but our arms around each other.

ACKNOWLEDGMENTS

Grateful acknowledgment is made to the editors of the publications in which the following poems first appeared, some in slightly different form:

Ayris Magazine: "Motel"
The Carolina Quarterly: "When They Ask About My Face"
Cirque: "Controlled Flight into Terrain"
Fjords: "Ajar," "Boats in Stasis"
The Gettysburg Review: "The Human Double Helix Does Not Spiral Infinitely," "Of a Thousand Other Things That Turn Up," "Reincarnation"
The Journal: "Echolocation," "Naming"
The Los Angeles Review: "In Which I Explain to You About the Tongue"
The MacGuffin: "Aubade at Seaside, Rent into Fourteen Lines"
New Fraktur Arts Journal: "Quench"
Nimrod: "Box of Rocks"
Noctua Review: "Snow Is Accumulating Rapidly," "Yellow"
P.Q. Leer: "Grief"
Paper Nautilus: "And Now My Mother Again"
The Pinch: "Anywhere, DST"
Potomac Review: "Adam: The Sequel"
Salamander: "Arcs of Detachment," "In the Beginning"
Sugar House Review: "Ablution"
The Summerset Review: "Suite: House, Storm"
Tiger's Eye: "And the Wren Bears to Her Nest Another Twig," "Permanence Being Art Not Science," "Scripture"
Whistling Shade: "Mill Creek at Plainville"
The William and Mary Review: "Spring Boulevard"

"After the Churn" first appeared in *Original Weather* (Uttered Chaos, 2011), an anthology of mixed-media works on paper by Robert Tomlinson accompanied by poems written to each work.

"I'm Not Like You Think I Am" first appeared in the anthology, *Turn* (Uttered Chaos, 2013).

"And Now My Mother Again" was reprinted as "I Dream My Mother Again" in *BILiNE: Best Indie Lit New England, Volume 2* (Black Key Press, 2015).

Deep appreciation to my writing companions, the 1st & 3rd Poets, for all the joyful years of table time and scrupulous critique. Abundant thanks to Laura Kasischke for her generous spirit, and my gratitude to Colette Jonopulos, who keeps the votives flickering. Quinton Hallett's poems and hand and heart informed and enkindled this manuscript; I am blessed with her friendship. A huge thank you to my editor, Diane Kistner, for her careful eye and unflagging support. And I am beyond grateful for Marcela Castañeda, who makes certain that someone is always home.

Cover artwork, "Still Life before an Open Window, Place Ravignan," by Juan Gris; author photo by Marcela Castañeda; cover and interior book design by Diane Kistner; Liberation Serif text and Sava Pro titling

About FutureCycle Press

FutureCycle Press is dedicated to publishing lasting English-language poetry books, chapbooks, and anthologies in both print-on-demand and Kindle ebook formats. Founded in 2007 by long-time independent editor/publishers and partners Diane Kistner and Robert S. King, the press incorporated as a nonprofit in 2012. A number of our editors are distinguished poets and writers in their own right, and we have been actively involved in the small press movement going back to the early seventies.

The FutureCycle Poetry Book Prize and honorarium is awarded annually for the best full-length volume of poetry we publish in a calendar year. Introduced in 2013, our Good Works projects are anthologies devoted to issues of universal significance, with all proceeds donated to a related worthy cause. Our Selected Poems series highlights contemporary poets with a substantial body of work to their credit; with this series we strive to resurrect work that has had limited distribution and is now out of print.

We are dedicated to giving all of the authors we publish the care their work deserves, making our catalog of titles the most diverse and distinguished it can be, and paying forward any earnings to fund more great books.

We've learned a few things about independent publishing over the years. We've also evolved a unique, resilient publishing model that allows us to focus mainly on vetting and preserving for posterity poetry collections of exceptional quality without becoming overwhelmed with bookkeeping and mailing, fundraising activities, or taxing editorial and production "bubbles." To find out more about what we are doing, come see us at www.futurecycle.org.

THE FUTURECYCLE POETRY BOOK PRIZE

All full-length volumes of poetry published by FutureCycle Press in a given calendar year are considered for the annual FutureCycle Poetry Book Prize. This allows us to consider each submission on its own merits, outside of the context of a contest. Too, the judges see the finished book, which will have benefitted from the beautiful book design and strong editorial gloss we are famous for.

The book ranked the best in judging is announced as the prizewinner in the subsequent year. There is no fixed monetary award; instead, the winning poet receives an honorarium of 20% of the total net royalties from all poetry books and chapbooks the press sold online in the year the winning book was published. The winner is also accorded the honor of being on the panel of judges for the next year's competition; all judges receive copies of all contending books to keep for their personal library.

www.ingramcontent.com/pod-product-compliance
Lightning Source LLC
Chambersburg PA
CBHW070009100426
42741CB00012B/3164